The Milkmaid

Randolph Caldecott's

Picture

BOOKS

[ZHINGOORA BOOKS]

This digital edition is published by
Zhingoora Books.

The Cover is Designed by Pallav Sethiya.

A Lady said to her Son—a poor young Squire:

"You must seek a Wife with a Fortune!"

"Where are you going, my Pretty Maid?"

"I'm going a-milking, Sir," she said.

"Shall I go with you, my Pretty Maid?"

"Oh yes, if you please, kind Sir," she said.

"What is your Father, my Pretty Maid?"

"My Father's a Farmer, Sir," she said.

"Shall I marry you, my Pretty Maid?"

"Oh thank you, kindly, Sir," she said.

"But what is your fortune, my pretty Maid?"

"My face is my fortune, Sir," she said.

"Then I can't marry you, my Pretty Maid!"

"Nobody asked you, Sir!" she said.

"Nobody asked you, Sir!" she said.

"Sir!" she said.

"Nobody asked you, Sir!" she said.

The End